BRITISH ROADS
OXFORDSHIRE
PAST AND PRESENT

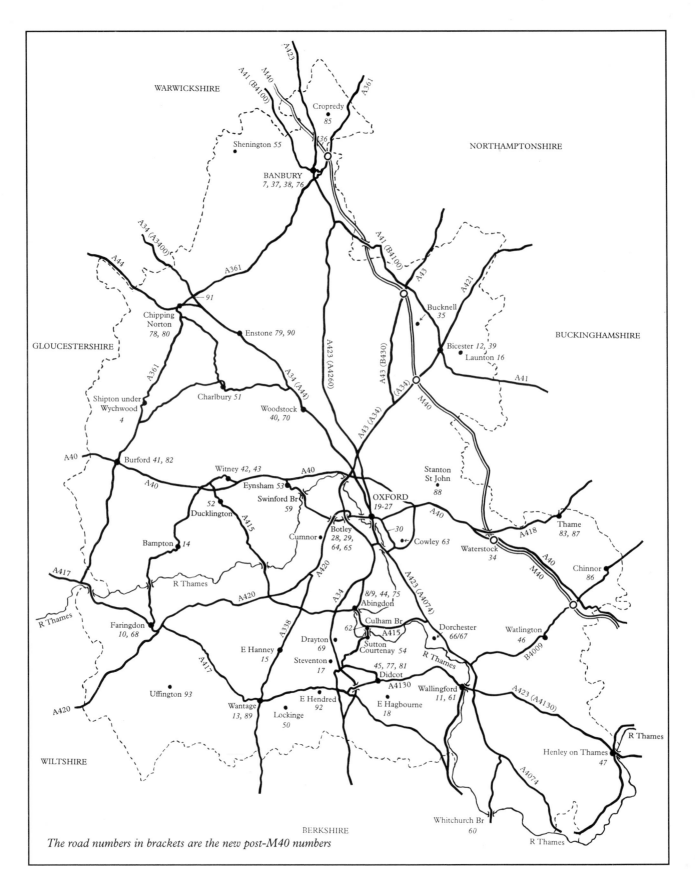

The road numbers in brackets are the new post-M40 numbers

This map shows the county's major roads together with other routes and locations featured in the book.
The numbers in *italics* refer to page numbers where the appropriate illustration may be found.

BRITISH ROADS

OXFORDSHIRE

PAST AND PRESENT

A nostalgic look at
the county's highways and byways

Susan Clark

Past & Present Publishing Ltd

SHIPTON UNDER WYCHWOOD: A 1949 scene in this delightful Oxfordshire location - outside the Shaven Crown Hotel is a solitary car, possibly a Vauxhall, while the postman on his rural cycle delivery somewhat self-consciously leans on his bike. He may be on his way to the village post office, then located in Church Street, by the war memorial in the distance. Stop lines marked on the road, like the one shown here, were first introduced in the 1930s. The direction sign would have been quite new, a replacement for the one removed during the Second World War. *Crown Copyright*

Any postman loitering on this spot in 1993 would be taking his life in his hands, as would any driver parking outside the hotel. The 'STOP' roadmarkings are now much more prominent. Though roadsigns were redesigned in the 1960s in the name of legibility, it is hard to see how anyone could think this untidy tangle an improvement on the earlier arrangement. It's interesting to note that the Shaven Crown Hotel's allegiance to the RAC seems to have lapsed, and that Ascott under Wychwood has moved a quarter of a mile further away.

Contents

First published in September 1993

British Library Cataloguing in Publication Data

A catalogue record for this book is available from the British Library.

ISBN 1 85895 012 0

Past & Present Publishing Ltd
Unit 5
Home Farm Close
Church Street
Wadenhoe
Peterborough PE8 5TE
Tel/fax (08015) 4 4 0

Printed and bound in Great Britain

All present-day photographs were taken by the author

Photographs credited 'OPA' are reproduced by permission of Oxfordshire Photographic Archive, Centre for Oxfordshire Studies (see page 96).

Map drawn by Christina Siviter

Introduction and acknowledgements

*R*oads are the skeleton of our land, the framework around which our settlements were founded, grow and thrive or decline and fade away. Yet they are not just part of our dim history. Read any local newspaper or listen to the local radio station and you will realise what strong feelings are provoked by any changes to our road system. Almost every day we hear of a new campaign for a bypass or against the building of a new road, a public protest about an accident black spot, a complaint about the inconvenience of road humps or demands for cheaper parking or more cycle tracks. In short, roads are an important part of the fabric of our lives.

Oxfordshire, because of its geographical position, is at the heart of Britain's network of roads, a network which has grown up over many centuries from a rich mixture of tracks and footpaths, packhorse and drovers' roads, trade routes, Roman roads, coaching routes, military highways and turnpike roads. Its prominence as a major Thames crossing point put Oxford at the centre of the county's system, with many of the major roads radiating out from it, like the spokes of a wheel. Since the coming of the county's newest road, the M40 extension in 1991, some of these 'spokes' have been given new and unfamiliar numbers. And not only the roads have changed - the counties have too. For the sake of simplicity, the Oxfordshire roads, towns and villages described here lie within the post-1974 boundary and include those which were incorporated into the county from northern Berkshire in that year.

It has not been my intention in this book to trace the route of each road and the towns and villages along it. Rather, I have grouped photographs together according to subject matter or theme, in what I hope is an interesting - and not too eclectic - manner. For many of the 'past and present' comparisons I have had to rely on that most fallible of faculties, memory - usually my own. Please forgive me if I have misremembered or misinterpreted facts. My excuse is that I have only lived in the county for the past twenty years.

Writing a book of this kind is a sort of journey, and on this trip I have learned many things. My admiration for the beauty and quirkiness of 'my' county has been redoubled and, as a bonus, I have discovered some hidden corners and heard some fascinating stories of which, to my shame, I had been ignorant in the past. I have learned to travel prepared, kitted out not only with a camera, maps and notebooks, but also with a brush, a bucket and a damp cloth to sweep up litter and wash down dirty roadsigns. As a travelling road detective, I have had to learn to drive safely with only one eye on the road, while the other searched around for useful reference points. And I almost learned how to master a map.

It wasn't all plain driving, however. As a road photographer, I hit some unexpected snags. Time after time I found it impossible to recreate the exact angle of the 'past' photograph, because in the intervening years a bridge had been inconveniently demolished, a rutted country track had been transformed into a busy four-lane dual carriageway, or a new office block had been built in the way. On a couple of occasions I accidentally timed my arrival at a picturesque village to coincide with the dustbin men, so that every thatched cottage or country pub had its black bin-bags or battered dustbins outside. And the least said about the unpredictability of the weather, the better.

The changes that have taken place on our roads since the war have been momentous. Almost every household now owns what many of our parents and grandparents would have rated as an unobtainable luxury - a car. And we rightly treasure the freedom that it gives us. Yet no one can view the tarmacking of yet more open countryside and increasing city-centre congestion with complacency. To use an apt metaphor, we are reaching a crossroads in our motoring history. Who knows what the next fifty years will bring?

But this isn't a study of the social implications of British transport. It's simply a glance back over our shoulders at a time when parking was no problem and no one had even heard of 'sleeping policemen'. I hope you enjoy our trip down Oxfordshire's Memory Lanes.

The majority of the 'past' photographs in this book came from the Oxfordshire Photographic Archive - 'OPA' in the picture credits. My thanks to them for their help and for the many happy hours I spent browsing through history. My special thanks to Don Stoneham for access to both his colour slides of Witney and his extensive local knowledge. I would also like to thank the following for their assistance with the preparation of this book:

David Frost; John Weal; Chris Hill; Clive Fewins; Loraine Fergusson; Louise Esplin; Pamela Woodage, who looks after her late husband Peter's collection; The Bodleian Library; Sir William Halcrow & Partners Ltd; Department of Transport, and in particular The Director, South East Construction Programme Division; Royal Automobile Club; The Post Office; various Oxfordshire Tourist Information Centres; MG Car Club; Heritage Motor Centre, Gaydon; National Motor Museum, Beaulieu; Oxfordshire County Council, in particular the Department of Planning & Property Services and the County Engineer's Department; Morland & Co plc; Rover Cars; and my unofficial personal car-spotter, Michael Clark.

1. Market places

BANBURY: 13 July 1961, and Banbury Market Place is a mass of parked cars. In their centre is the well-known white-on-blue 'P' parking sign, first used in this country in the 1930s. Parking is so dense that it almost seems to be blocking access to and from the side roads. Among the many popular car models of the time pictured here are a Rover, an Austin A40 van, a Ford Anglia and a Ford Popular. The tall overhanging concrete street-lights are also typical of the decade. *OPA*

Thirty years later and Banbury Market Place is still a crowded car park. But today it has a more orderly look and drivers must pay and display. Fancy herringbone paving has replaced the painted tarmac of the 'sixties and there is pedestrian access only to the High Street, cutting down on congestion in the Market Place.

Left ABINGDON Market Place, for centuries the hub of life in the town, is also little more than a car park in this picture taken in the 1950s, at the beginning of the postwar motoring boom. Among the specimens of vehicles seen here are a Morris Minor convertible and a Triumph Mayflower. Note the early forerunner of the modern bike-rack on the left and, also on the left, the decorative brickwork of The Queens Hotel. The hotel was one of several buildings demolished when Bury Street shopping precinct was constructed as part of the town centre redevelopment in the 1960s. A second pub, an Usher's house, is on the extreme right. *RCHME Crown Copyright*

The only vehicles you'll see in Abingdon Market Place these days are authorised to be there, such as those belonging to stall-holders at the busy Monday market. Pedestrians can stroll or sit in peaceful traffic-free conditions. Four replica Victorian lamps have replaced the ones shown in the 1950s picture. The café of the 'fifties was later turned into a public house, called The Queens in memory of the old hotel, and is now a fashion store. Ironically, in recent years the shopping precinct has itself been criticised as being outmoded and unattractive and moves have been made to have it modernised.

Above Market Squares are also used for more frivolous purposes. This is Abingdon Fair in October 1957, held in and around the Market Place, and followed every year by a smaller event, known as the Runaway Fair. Both have their origins in Michaelmas hiring fairs. The children or even grandchildren of the youngsters pictured here may still enjoy the fun of the fair, as the tradition continues today as strongly as ever. *OPA*

Below Attempts were made to ban vehicles from parking in the Market Place after the pedestrian shopping precinct was created. This proved difficult to enforce until the special Abingdon Market Place Act came into being in 1978.

FARINGDON: This was the scene in August 1979 from beneath the stone pillars of the 17th-century Town Hall in the Market Place, looking towards Marlborough Street. A month before this picture was taken the town's bypass was opened, greatly reducing traffic through the town. In the years before then, heavy traffic between Swindon and Oxford had been pounding Faringdon's narrow streets, and traffic lights were installed to help control the flow. 'No entry' signs bar access to traffic turning right into Gloucester Street. *OPA*

After the opening of the bypass, there was no longer a need for traffic signals and these were subsequently removed. Flower-tubs now stand in their place and the ugly control box has disappeared. There have been other improvements too - beneath the Town Hall the uneven paving has been replaced, and the clock missing from the background of the earlier picture is back in its rightful place. The one-way system along Marlborough Street and Gloucester Street remains in action and a simple 'All traffic' sign has replaced the earlier directional sign. Double yellow 'no loading' lines prevent parking.

WALLINGFORD Market Place on a sunny day in November 1980. In the foreground is a Victorian drinking fountain, given to the town by Alderman Hawkins in 1885; his shop used to overlook the market. The fountain originally stood in the Market Place but was moved to the Bullcroft, a local park, for some years. It was returned to its present spot in 1979. In the background, a road running in front of it, is the Town Hall, which dates from 1670, with a war memorial in front. *OPA*

The is the same setting in 1993, on a Friday when it was busy with market-day shoppers and the drinking fountain was almost hidden amongst the market stalls. I wonder if Alderman Hawkins would approve of having a line of underpants strung from his gift? There has been some easing of the traffic situation through the centre of Wallingford since the opening of a bypass early in 1993. The Town Hall and war memorial in the background are unchanged, though the church has lost its turrets.

BICESTER: Town centre traffic in the 1960s had to negotiate through a very confined space at the southern end of Sheep Street, where it meets Market Square. The problem was the Hedges building, which stood very close to what was then Hilton's shoes, just visible on the extreme right-hand side of this picture, taken in March 1963. Cars and heavier vehicles had to squeeze through the gap, often mounting the pavement and damaging buildings. Something had to be done. *OPA*

This view of Market Square in Bicester from a different angle shows it on 18 May 1963, after the demolition of the Hedges building; Hilton's is on the left. The road is now clear and two-way traffic is able to pass freely. The hope was that this new wide road would speed traffic through the town. *OPA*

The same scene thirty years later, and Hilton's is now an estate agent. In the 1990s it is not generally regarded as a good idea to have traffic speeding through a town centre, so the road width has now been restricted artificially with lane markings! Some of the road space is taken up by a taxi-rank and traffic is once again one-way. So much for progress.

WANTAGE Market Place in 1958: King Alfred surveys a collection of cars; from left to right, a Ford Anglia, a Morris Minor, a Ford Consul Mk 2 (to the right of the statue) and a 1940s Morris M type can be identified. On the right is a group of Lambretta scooters. Vespa and Lambretta were the most popular scooter models in the 'fifties and 'sixties and became as much a fashion accessory as a means of transport. An early Tesco store, more modest than the superstores we are used to today, can be seen in the background. *Peter Townsend*

King Alfred still presides over rows of parked cars, but the scene is subtly different. Black concrete bollards have been erected round the Market Place, limiting access for vehicles, and seats and litter-bins surround the royal figure. Though it is still free, parking time in the Market Place is limited to 30 minutes. Increased traffic has meant the introduction of pelican crossings with their zigzag lines for pedestrians.

BAMPTON Market Square in the 1950s looks the epitome of a sleepy old town. No people are in sight and there's very little sign of traffic. The Town Hall stands alone in the centre of the quiet square, half hidden behind trees, with the war memorial to the right. You can almost hear the silence. *OPA*

To the modern driver, wide open spaces in a town centre mean only one thing: somewhere to park. Essentially unchanged, but inevitably cluttered with vehicles, this is the same square four decades later. Part of the road has been made into a car park and in it stands a row of bottle-banks. Parked cars line the street. The Town Hall clock towers seem to have become a casualty of the passing years, though the war memorial now boasts a neat surrounding kerb.

2. Village scenes

EAST HANNEY lies close to the crossroads where the road to Steventon meets the A338, Wantage to Oxford road; this was a dangerous junction with a long history of road accidents when this photograph was taken in 1981. In the triangle of grass in the foreground stand two magnificent horse chestnut trees with their girdle of seats, and in the background a farmhouse has been converted into a restaurant. *OPA*

In 1993 the triangle of grass, the trees and the seating remain the same, but the layout has seen some changes in the name of road safety. Early in the 'nineties the junction was staggered, with the Steventon road offset to the south. The redundant spur of road, still with its twin streetlights beside it, now only gives access to the Italian restaurant. Black and white chevrons draw the change to motorists' attention, and new directional signs and an unmissable 'STOP' sign have been erected.

Even more changes to the Steventon road are in prospect if Thames Water's proposed huge new reservoir between Abingdon and Wantage gets the go-ahead. It would leave the present road under millions of gallons of water, so it is planned to realign it further to the south.

View showing Post Office, Launton.

LAUNTON: This is Station Road in Launton village near Bicester as it was some thirty years ago. At the cross-roads there's an old-style 'Halt at Major Road Ahead' sign, probably dating back to the 1950s. No streetlighting is apparent and power lines are strung across the road. Outside the post office and village stores is a Vauxhall, and across the road a Hillman. On the pavement on the left-hand side a child has abandoned its tricycle. *OPA*

The same street today, with a modern octagonal 'STOP' sign replacing the old one. Streetlighting has now been provided, but the untidy power lines are still there. A relatively elderly but still elegant Mercedes Benz is in the foreground; maybe the owner is patronising the Auto Parts shop, next door to the now defunct post office.

STEVENTON: The main British Rail line from Swindon to Didcot and London passes to the south of Steventon, crossing village streets at two points less than a quarter of a mile apart. This is Causeway Level Crossing (the other is Stocks Lane). Until the early 1970s Causeway Crossing was equipped with swinging gates operated manually by the crossing-keeper. He, or in this case she, was housed in the wooden crossing cabin, complete with its own chimney. *OPA*

Warning lights and automatic barriers were installed at Causeway in 1972, controlled by the crossing-keeper in a new high-tech cabin. The keeper here also controls the level crossing at Stocks Lane, using cameras and closed circuit television to monitor the road. The new barriers are operated by merely pressing buttons. This was the scene with the barriers closed to road traffic on 22 February 1993.

EAST HAGBOURNE: The main street in East Hagbourne with its butcher's shop looked like this on 13 October 1977. Although white lines began to be painted on our roads as early as the First World War, by the 1970s they still had not reached village roads such as this one. A VW 'Beetle' is one of the parked cars. *OPA*

   Remarkably little has changed in this part of East Hagbourne by 1993; even the butcher's shop is still there. Hedges and trees have grown, of course, and the centre line of the road is now marked. It's also been found necessary to stop nuisance parking on the grass verges by putting in white bollards. The Methodist Chapel, whose roof can just be glimpsed above the shop frontage, is now a private home.

Oxford: coping with traffic in an historic city

In the Middle Ages, antagonism between the students and townspeople of Oxford erupted into violence, known as the Town and Gown riots. Today Oxford is struggling with another conflict of interests, and this one could well be dubbed Town versus Traffic. How this conflict will end, and who - if anyone - will be the winner, may well be decided in the next ten years.

Oxford's traffic problems are far from unique - just about every historic town and city from Gloucester to Edinburgh or Norwich to Nottingham has had to take steps to save itself from being swamped by the ever-increasing transport demands of the 20th century. Even new towns like Milton Keynes have discovered that they can't cope with traffic levels that have soared beyond anyone's expectations.

For decades the situation in central Oxford has been recognised as inefficient, unhealthy and unpleasant, and various attempts have been made to improve it. Now Oxfordshire County Council has gone all out to solve the problems by commissioning independent consultants to make a one-year study and put forward proposals to free Oxford of its traffic nightmare. The report was

completed in 1992, and the first phases are now beginning to be implemented.

Put simply, there are only two ways of unclogging urban traffic congestion: you can increase the capacity of the roads, or decrease the amount of car traffic and in the process encourage other means of transport, like buses, bikes or good old-fashioned walking. In the forty or more years that Oxford has been

Cornmarket Street today, semi-pedestrianised and crowded with shoppers and buses, and how it could look after full pedestrianisation.

grappling with its problem, it has tried various schemes and combinations of schemes to achieve these ends, none of them completely successful in the long run.

The construction of a ring road round the city in the 1970s didn't prove the panacea it was hoped, as most of the city centre traffic was found to be local, not passing through. Building new roads through the centre was another idea put forward. This was eventually ruled out, because it would have entailed demolishing a number of architecturally important buildings or cutting through the beauty spots of the University Parks and Christ Church Meadow. For a time it seemed as though the situation had been contained, if not solved, by the balanced transport policy pioneered by the city in the 'seventies and 'eighties.

A mixture of schemes including 'park and ride', bus lanes, cycle lanes, parking controls and partial pedestrianisation was used to entice motorists to leave their cars outside the city centre. In fact, though the number of people travelling to the centre has grown considerably in the last 25 years, the amount of car traffic has remained constant. But with bus deregulation in the 1980s, bus congestion was added to the problems and it became clear that further, more drastic steps were needed.

So what does the new transport study say? In a nutshell, the strategy is to put pedestrians and cyclists first. Cornmarket Street, one of the main shopping streets, will be fully pedestrianised instead of the present partial system, and there will be a daytime ban on private through traffic in the High Street and St Aldates. A 'bus gate' will be installed at the eastern end of the High Street, which will use cameras and sensors to detect unauthorised car traffic. Once the car traffic has been decreased - and they are aiming for an 80 per cent reduction - there will be more space for buses and bikes. Already, almost one in five trips within the city is made by bike, and it is hoped to increase this number by provid-

Broad Street as it looks at the moment, with cars parked down the centre and along the kerb, and again as it could be with an ancient monument, the Carfax Conduit, erected on the grassed central area.

ing more cycle lanes, routes and stands. Sticks and carrots - in the form of even more restricted parking and better 'park and ride' and public transport services - will be used to persuade more people to abandon private cars. And once traffic levels have been reduced, it is hoped that the way will be open to introduce further pedestrianisation. Of course there have been objections to the plan, mostly from traders worried about losing customers, but on the whole the County Council has found the local people to be enthusiastically behind the changes.

More efficient public transport is clearly the key to solving many city-centre transport problems. Oxford's study showed that already 30 per cent of people travel to the city centre by bus. But, useful though they are, buses are now in danger of choking the life of the city by creating congestion and diesel pollution. The Oxford scheme calls for 'bus taming' - buses will be better managed, re-routed if necessary and, where possible, replaced by more environmentally friendly vehicles. Battery-powered and hybrid-powered buses, which can switch from battery to diesel according to

the circumstances, are both likely to be seen in service in Oxford soon.

These are commonsense, unspectacular measures which it is hoped can be introduced step by step without causing dramatic changes or sudden disruptions to the life of the city. Yet, added together, they could mean salvation for central Oxford and its long-suffering inhabitants - and ultimately could lead the way to similar improvements in other historic cities. By the year 2000 we should know whether these measures have succeeded in recreating in the centre of Oxford conditions that befit one of Europe's foremost historic cities.

All illustrations courtesy of Oxfordshire County Council

St Giles at present, with parked cars and narrow pavements, and as it could be under the new scheme.

3. In and around Oxford

CARFAX: In 1953, as now, Carfax was the heart of Oxford's city centre. Even then traffic was quite heavy, with bicycles and pedestrians especially numerous. Traffic lights at the crossroads controlled access to the High, St Aldates, Queen Street and Cornmarket. Transport buffs should be able to identify a Morris van, a Hillman, a Vauxhall, a Morris 8, and an AEC bus, among others. *BR/OPC Collection*

The more recent photograph, taken from a first-floor office window on 11 March 1993, shows just what a traffic problem Oxford city centre is up against. Carfax is one of the most congested and polluted parts of the city: buses and cars clog the roads, and pedestrians swarm across the pavements. In the 1970s the road layout was altered in an attempt to deal with the increased traffic. The entrance to Queen Street, to the left of Carfax Tower, was narrowed and the road partially pedestrianised; repairs to the pavement were being done when this photo was taken. But workers, shoppers and tourists still have to dodge the many buses and taxis that have access. Queen Street is just one of the problem areas highlighted in the recent study of Oxford's city centre transport described in the preceding pages.

HIGH STREET: This is the view from Longwall Street along the High, with Queen's College in the centre, as it looked in 1962. Traffic is passing freely, delivery vans can park and the cyclist has plenty of room. Two popular vehicles of the time can be seen - a Minivan is turning right into Queen's Lane and heading towards us is a 'bubble car'. These strange-looking runabouts were imported in the 'fifties, and several variations were manufactured by companies like Isetta, Messerschmidt, Daf and General Motors. This one appears to be a Heinkel three-wheeler, two-seater model. *OPA*

In the 1990s the picture is quite different. It's almost impossible to appreciate the architectural beauty of the High, as it's so congested. Tourist buses cruise the streets: 'Every 15 minutes, every day' boasts the slogan. Cycle lanes have been created to encourage Oxford's cyclists and there is a pelican crossing. The Oxford Transport Study proposes to go further and close the High to through traffic during the daytime, except for buses and cycles.

RADCLIFFE SQUARE: In December 1973 Radcliffe Square looked like this. One of Oxford's many cycles is casually leaning against the railings, while an MG sports car and others are parked beneath one of the last gas-lamps left in the city; in fact, the very last gas-lamp wasn't turned off until 1979. On the right is the round Radcliffe Camera, and behind it in the background is the spire of St Mary's Church. *OPA*

Even in this timeless corner of Oxford, 20th century commercialism discreetly rears its head in the 1990s - the stall does a good trade selling souvenir T-shirts. Some time in the last twenty years the gas-lamp has been replaced and the railings removed. Yellow lines have appeared and hefty barriers and bollards bar traffic entering the square from Catte Street. The area is still littered with bikes, sometimes piled high on top of each other, though these days you are more likely to find a colourful mountain bike than this 'sit up and beg' model with its basket. And today all the bikes are securely chained and padlocked.

CUTTESLOWE: Roads may be blocked for many reasons, but the case of the Cutteslowe Walls must be one of the strangest road closures in modern history. These so-called 'snob walls' were built in 1934 in a northern suburb of Oxford across two sets of roads, to separate private from council residents: a sort of suburban Berlin Wall. During their controversial existence, the case reached the High Court and the walls were demolished and rebuilt several times - sometimes on the same day. But despite great publicity, many demonstrations and appeals, it wasn't until 1959 that they were knocked down for good. *OPA*

The seven-foot-tall buttressed walls with spikes on the top cut abruptly across two sets of roads - Wolsey and Carlton Roads and Wentworth and Aldrich Roads - and continued across the footpath and into the front gardens of the adjoining houses. This is the wall between Wolsey and Carlton Roads, as seen from the 'council side' on the day of demolition in March 1959. A party of local councillors is there to witness the eventual triumph of commonsense. *OPA*

Today there is no trace of the walls, except the abrupt change of road name and architecture. Looking at this ordinary domestic scene - the former 'council side' - it is hard to imagine the high emotions that were stirred up during the prolonged dispute. Since the taking down of the walls, many of the local authority houses have been privately bought and now both sections of the estate look equally prosperous, with replacement windows and smart cars outside.

From the opposite direction, this is all that is left to remind us of the Cutteslowe Wall in Carlton/Wolsey Road - a sturdy wooden fence and high hedge in a front garden (left). Is it too fanciful to suggest that these robust boundaries indicate the territorial instincts of modern Cutteslowe inhabitants are as strong as ever?

WEST WAY, BOTLEY, as it looked from the Botley Road in July 1967, ten years before the bypass. Traffic is sparse over Botley Bridge and the road markings minimal. To the left is the George public house, and beside it the old-style roadsign directing traffic straight on and to the right. In the centre background is Seacourt Tower, which was officially opened in October 1966. *OPA*

   Twenty-six years on and West Way, despite Oxford's Southern Bypass, is jammed with traffic, most of it local. A bus lane marked on the road leads to a 'park and ride' car park. But even with the improvements, this part of Oxford during the rush hour is not a place to drive through unless you have to. Some mornings it can take up to 25 minutes to crawl from West Way along Botley Road to Oxford railway station - a distance of a mile. A new road-sign directs all through traffic to the right for the Oxford ring road or the A420 to Swindon and Bristol.

BOTLEY SOUTHERN BYPASS: From a high vantage point, this was the view over the Botley Roundabout on 14 October 1977, not long after the interchange was opened in August of that year. Even though it has been in operation for several weeks, the junction is strangely quiet with only a few vehicles, including a Morris Traveller and an ERF lorry. *OPA*

This slightly different view of the roundabout was taken from the 9th floor of Seacourt Tower in 1993. A roadworks sign almost in the centre of the picture refers to work on the nearby Botley flyover. The flyover has not proved as durable as it should have done and a four-month project is under way to completely rebuild it - needless to say, this will cause considerable disruption and long delays to traffic.

The houses in the foreground of the earlier photograph have gone and the roofs you can now see belong to several superstores which have been built on the site.

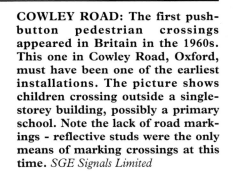

COWLEY ROAD: The first push-button pedestrian crossings appeared in Britain in the 1960s. This one in Cowley Road, Oxford, must have been one of the earliest installations. The picture shows children crossing outside a single-storey building, possibly a primary school. Note the lack of road markings - reflective studs were the only means of marking crossings at this time. *SGE Signals Limited*

An updated pelican crossing in exactly the same busy place is today in use every couple of minutes. In the background the two-storey buildings have survived the decades, though the shop frontages have changed - probably many times. The single-storey building and the wall have made way for a Boots supermarket.

Cowley Road in the 1990s is a lively, cosmopolitan shopping and restaurant area in east Oxford. In a newsagent's window near where this photo was taken was a postcard advertising a room in 'a chilled-out students' house'.

The Cowley Car Plant - from Morris Minor to Rover 600

It was in 1912 that William Morris, a pioneer in British car-making, decided that his premises in Longwall Street, Oxford, were too cramped. So he set up car production in a disused military college just outside Oxford in Cowley. Seventy-one years later, cars are still being made at the Cowley plant. And Lord Nuffield's office (as Morris later became) is there too, preserved as it was when he died in 1963.

Instead of the 'Bullnose' Morris Oxford, with which Cowley's car production began, the modern factory produces Maestros and Montegos, as well as the Rover 800 series, Britain's best-selling executive car in 1992, and, since 1993, the Rover 600 series.

The Second World War brought car manufacture all over Britain almost to a standstill, but the industry picked up surprisingly quickly afterwards. It was a time of rapid growth, as manufacturers saw the potential of supplying cars to everyone, not just to the wealthier middle classes. British car-makers were eager to try out new technical and design ideas that they had developed during the stagnant wartime years. They also began to look to Europe and across the Atlantic for their markets. It was then that Morris launched what was to prove to be the most long-lived British car of all, the homely Morris Minor.

It was produced at Cowley and designed by Alec Issigonis, later to become even more famous as the designer of the Mini. Its performance was modest, with a top speed of 62 mph, but it sold and sold. In fact, the Morris Minor, still with its 'poached egg' design, stayed in production from 1948 until 1971 and in all 1.6 million were produced.

In 1948 there were only two major, truly British car manufacturers, Austin and Morris. In 1952 came the first of many mergers, reorganisations and name changes that have characterised the British motor industry over the decades. The Nuffield Organisation, which included Morris, merged with its rival, the Austin Motor Company of Longbridge, to form the British Motor Corporation (BMC), producing MG, Riley and Wolseley cars, as well as Austins and Morrises.

In the 'fifties and 'sixties BMC grew to be Britain's biggest car-maker, rivalled in this country only by Ford. Credit for much of the company's success during the 1960s can be traced to one model, the BMC Mini, launched in 1959. At first Cowley's version was known as the Morris Mini-Minor but, along with the skirts of the young women of the time, the name was soon shortened.

The impact this compact little car had is hard to exaggerate. Again we have the genius of Alec Issigonis to thank for the design, which popularised and combined the concepts of the transverse engine and front-wheel drive. Though only ten feet long, four adults could be fitted in and in 1959 it cost just £537. More than five million Austin and Morris Minis have been produced at Cowley and Longbridge since 1959, and the car is still being made at Longbridge.

A 1949 Morris Minor pictured outside an Oxfordshire hotel. The Minor became Britain's longest-produced model.

The 1962 Mini production line at Cowley, with ADO 10 bodies for Westminsters or Wolseleys on the right.

cial backing. More name changes resulted, with Cowley eventually becoming part of the Austin Rover Group.

The happy products of this reorganisation were the Austin Metro, Maestro and Montego ranges, though only the last two were - and still are - produced at the Oxfordshire plant. Together, 'the three Ms' spelt out recovery for the company. Collaboration with the Japanese firm Honda led to the Triumph Acclaim being built at Cowley, and later the Rover 800 series. In 1986 Cowley workers had to get used to yet another name change, as the company became simply Rover Group. Production of Rover cars is now concentrated at only two main sites, Cowley and Longbridge, and history turned full circle in 1988 when Rover Group was denationalised and sold to British Aerospace.

Bringing the Cowley story up to date, the sprawling collection of buildings that once made up the plant has been consolidated into one main 'super-site', where the whole production process from raw materials to completed cars takes place. In 1993, in the largest civil engineering project ever undertaken in the UK, the North and South Works were demolished and a distinctive Cowley landmark, the conveyor bridge over the Oxford Ring Road, was pulled down (see page 63). This left a slimmed-down site of just 112 acres, by comparison with the 222 acres it used to cover. Over the years the workforce has been streamlined too, with fewer employees making fewer cars, but aiming them at the higher end of the market. In the 'sixties, when employment at Cowley was at its peak, the workforce numbered 11,000; now it's 5,000.

Rover has invested £200 million in the new plant, which is capable of producing 110,000 cars a year. The hope is that with one of the most compact and flexible plants in Europe, the long history of car-making at Cowley will continue securely into the future.

Later in the decade, another successful Issigonis design, the 1100, was produced at Cowley and remained for many years Britain's best-selling car. By the time production ceased in 1974, 2.1 million had been produced.

Despite these successes, towards the end of the decade BMC's fortunes were on the wane. In January 1968 another merger was announced, this time between Leyland and BMC (by then metamorphosed into BMH, British Motor Holdings), and the British Leyland Motor Corporation (BLMC or BL) was formed. The site at Cowley now found itself one of many BL factories all over Britain, producing a dozen different car marques, including Austin-Morris, Jaguar, Rover and Triumph.

The 'seventies brought a new threat to British car-making: the first of many imported Japanese cars began to appear on our roads. Cowley's answer to the increasing foreign competition was a series of popular family cars: the Maxi in 1969, the Morris Marina in 1971 and the Allegro in 1973.

The fuel crisis that followed the Arab-Israeli war in 1973 led to a lean time for car manufacturers. Japanese competition was by then beginning to present a serious challenge to British and European cars. By 1975 BL was virtually nationalised and received substantial government finan-

Above A lunchtime scene at Gate 8 of the Cowley factory on 2 November 1960, at a time of peak employment when 11,000 worked on the site.

Left A 1966 Morris Mini, built at Cowley - one of the five million produced since 1959.

All photographs courtesy of BMIHT/Rover Group except where indicated

Right A recent Rover radiator badge with its famous Viking longship. The Viking motif has been associated with Rover Cars since the 1920s, when a fearsome Viking warrior with winged helmet, axe and shield was used as a radiator mascot. By 1929 a less aggressive Viking ship emerged as the logo and this longship device has been in use ever since. Designs have varied over the years: sometimes there were extravagant blue waves, sometimes no waves at all, but one of the more constant features is the red sail. Until the 1970s the badge was enamel, and although commercial pressures mean that today's Rover badge is made of plastic, a complex manufacturing process ensures that it looks as impressive as ever. In fact, to Rover employees it is not a humble badge at all - within the company it is referred to as 'The Jewel'. *Author*

4. The M40 extension

Only one motorway crosses Oxfordshire - the M40, which extends for some 27 miles through the county. The southern half of the M40, junctions 1 to 7, joining London with Oxford, was completed in stages by 1974. The final section from Oxford to Birmingham, built at a cost of £293 million, was opened seventeen years later on 16 January 1991. The extension continues from Waterstock near Oxford, skirts round the city, Bicester and Banbury, and goes on through Warwickshire to connect with the M42 at Birmingham.

Already the volume of car and lorry traffic using the M40 has exceeded the level predicted. More than 77,600 vehicles a day have been counted at one point, and this increased traffic also puts pressure on other nearby roads. Already there's talk of major improvements being made to the A34 to increase its capacity. Is the M40 another example, like the M25 London orbital motorway, of the volume of traffic expanding to fill the amount of road available?

These aerial pictures, taken before and after construction work began, show how the Oxfordshire countryside was changed by the M40 extension.

WATERSTOCK: This is the starting point of the M40 extension. The first photograph shows the A40 as it looked in 1989, looking west towards Oxford. Two generations of roads are visible - the dual carriageway and, shadowing it on the right, the old London Road. At this time London Road was just a track leading to Holloway Farm, and ending in a curious 'B'-shaped section of road. Hedges mark the line of the disused Princes Risborough-Oxford railway across the top right-hand corner.

On 13 January 1991, three days before the M40 opened, this was the scene at the Waterstock intersection - to the other two, a third generation of roads has been added. The 'B'-shaped remnants of the old A40 and its successor, the A40 trunk road, are in the top left of the picture. But now, snaking between the farm buildings in empty six-lane splendour is the new motorway, veering northwards and crossed by three bridges. The nearest carries eastbound traffic from the A40(T) on to the motorway, the other two carry a footpath and the A418 over the motorway.

PAST AND PRESENT

BUCKNELL ROAD, looking north: Much of the M40 extension cut through open agricultural land like this. On 9 December 1988 the well-known landmark of Bucknell Water Tower stood sentinel in a field beside a quiet unclassified road leading to Bucknell village (population approximately 200). The only other noteworthy features are the triangle of woodland beside the road and, behind the water tower, a construction site. This is a clue to the future, for here Thames Water was deepening the water-main in preparation for the coming of the motorway.

In December 1990, almost exactly two years later, the area is transformed. The water tower overlooks the M40, still empty of traffic as it was not yet open. To get to the village, traffic now has to pass over Bucknell Bridge and an access track has been created beside the tower. The tower itself has been renovated and the water authority construction site grassed over. A corner of the foreground woodland has been sliced off by the motorway, but clearly discernable next it are traces of the old Bucknell Road, including the hedge that used to border it.

HARDWICK FARM BRIDGES, BANBURY: These three pictures give some insight into the construction problems faced by motorway engineers. You may find it difficult to orientate yourself at first, as it is almost impossible to take a series of aerial pictures from the same viewpoint.

Top The first picture shows the scene from the air, looking north-east from Banbury, in February 1988 just before work began. Crossing the top right-hand corner you can see the Daventry to Banbury road, and running north-south through the centre is the route of the dismantled Banbury-Woodford Halse railway line. On the left is the Oxford Canal with Hardwick Lock near the bend. Meandering beside it is the river Cherwell. Here, where the river and canal bend close to each other, was the place chosen for Hardwick Farm River and Canal Bridges.

Middle Only four months later and construction work on the bridges is well under way. This time we are looking in the opposite direction, south-west towards Banbury, so the canal is on the right and the river on the left. The Oxford Canal had to remain navigable at all times during the work and its waters diverted to accommodate the bridge. In this picture a hedge marks the old route.

To 'move' the canal and build the bridge, while keeping it open to river traffic, was a complicated procedure. It was achieved by building one bridge support, or abutment, on a dry site beside the canal and re-aligning the canal, lining its new route with steel sheet piles. The new route was then flooded, and the original site drained. This is the stage shown here, with the second abutment not yet built.

A different method was used for the River Cherwell. Its waters were diverted round the construction site before work on the box bridge began. In the distance is the Daventry Road Industrial Estate which lies to the north of Banbury. The Banbury to Oxford railway runs diagonally across the top right hand corner of the photograph, with a reservoir close by.

Bottom Finally, this is the same site from almost the same vantage point, again looking south-west, in July 1990, with the Banbury Bypass almost complete but not yet open. A dark 'C'-shape marks the old river bed of the Cherwell. The Daventry Road, just visible in the top left-hand corner of the photograph, is now truncated by the M40 and comes to a dead end. Thanks to some river signs, drivers passing along this section of the motorway can identify where it crosses the Cherwell.

All photographs courtesy of The Director, Department of Transport, South East Construction Programme Division

5. Town life

BANBURY has two claims to fame: its cross and its cakes. This is Banbury Cross as it looked almost twenty years ago, with West Bar behind it. Tourists hoping to get a closer look at the famous nursery rhyme cross at this time would have to brave the traffic surrounding it. In any case, this is not the original cross: that was pulled down by the Puritans in 1600. The present cross was erected in 1858 to celebrate the wedding of one of Queen Victoria's many daughters. Circling it on this day in 1975 are an Escort and a Hillman Avenger, among others. *OPA*

The cross has been cleaned and restored since the earlier photograph and the traffic island on which it stands enlarged, setting it at a more dignified distance from the traffic. It's no easier to get close up to, but at least flower-tubs add a little colour. In the background, some parking space has been lost and the pavement has been widened.

BANBURY is a fast-expanding Oxfordshire town, and has had to adapt to its growing population. One of the ways it has coped with increasing city-centre traffic is to create a pedestrianised area in the narrowest streets in the area of the High Street. Banbury High Street in January 1975 looked very different from today's scene. Pedestrians keep a wary eye open for traffic as they cross the long, straight street, while a Ford Cortina and an Escort are among the cars parked along the roadside. *OPA*

There are few such worries for pedestrians walking in the spring sunshine in the 1990s. From this point onwards the High Street is closed to traffic, as the roadsigns clearly indicate. In place of parked cars, there are broad pavements, seats and flowers, and even a modern bandstand. The line of shopfronts is today dominated by the stark lines of the new National Westminster Bank building, replacing the two shops shown on the right in the 1970s picture.

BICESTER: A young mother and her child cross Sheep Street in Bicester in 1957. At that time it was a wide thoroughfare, with plenty of room for roadside parking bays. Though the road is open and the only road marking is a white line on the bend, mother and pushchair can cross safely because of the scarcity of traffic. A Morris van and a Standard Triumph are stationary outside the shops. *OPA*

Contrast that with the 1993 scene. Would the modern mother and her youngster (this time travelling in the opposite direction) be able to cross with such confidence if this part of Sheep Street had it not been made into a pedestrian zone? Bicester is another fast-growing area - its population has grown by a third in the last ten years - and traffic pressure on the town centre has increased proportionally. But measures have been taken to help tip the balance in the pedestrian's favour. No vehicles, except buses, disabled drivers and deliveries, are allowed in this part of town during the day; pavements have been widened and roads narrowed, and there are traffic humps and frequent pedestrian crossings. In comparison with the 1950s scene, it's undoubtedly cluttered, but the shopper's safety and comfort are protected.

WOODSTOCK in the 1960s was already a tourist trap, and the roadsign at the Oxford Road crossroads indicates why. Blenheim Palace is right on its doorstep, and Stratford-upon-Avon (no doubt indicated on the unseen part of the sign) is just a short drive away. *OPA*

The new-style roadsigns certainly don't have the charm of the old finger-post, and they give directions to much more prosaic destinations than a palace and the Bard's birthplace. Pelican crossings have been introduced and a 'yellow box' junction has been marked on the road, to avoid the entrance to the High Street becoming blocked.

High St., Burford.

BURFORD's inhabitants are rightly proud of this view, and try hard to preserve it. The High Street, with its double line of pollarded limes, sweeps down into the Windrush valley to a little bridge. Apparently in the 1960s, when this was taken, drivers didn't need double yellow lines to remind them not to park on the hill. One car, an Austin 1100, probably belonging to a listed house in the High Street, parks on its driveway cut into the grass verge. *OPA*

If anything, three decades and many thousands of cars and visitors later, Burford High Street on 23 March 1993 looks even better, with its spring bulbs in bloom. A car stands on the drive in the same spot as before, but warning signs set in the grass prevent any unauthorised parking or driving on the grass verges (penalty £20). There have been some concessions to modern traffic conditions: double yellow lines and the centre road markings which allow overtaking only for traffic going down the hill. The streetlights have been replaced and sited on the other side of the road.

WITNEY: This 1961 picture shows the Town Hall on the left and part of the famous thirteen-pillared Buttercross, built in 1683, on the right. A yellow Ford Anglia is approaching the crossroads. The square stone building behind was originally an old coaching inn, the Crown. When it closed, part of the building was used by Frost's, the coal and coke merchant, and the other half by Habgood & Mammotts, auctioneers. To the left is a Co-op store. *Don Stoneham*

The Town Hall and Buttercross now frame a very different picture. The building known as Frost's has disappeared, demolished to make way for a new road, Langdale Gate, which links the town centre to Witan Way, an inner bypass. To the left, access is guarded by a gate that allows only specified traffic to pass, and the sign beside it gives details of the pedestrian zone which starts here and includes the new Woolgate Shopping Centre. The Co-op is now a supermarket. The sign warning of traffic humps refers to calming measures in the nearby High Street.

WITNEY: This is Corn Street as it looked in 1964. The road is gloriously free of parking restrictions and decorated with a colourful display of 1960s street advertising for Pepsi Cola, Bush electrical goods and Ecko radios. A line of bicycles is propped up on one side of the road, while outside the Eagle Tavern are a red Hillman Minx and a black Ford, possibly a Popular. At the far end of the street on the left, Tarrant's warehouse, a landmark in the town at the time, is being demolished. *Don Stoneham*

Tarrant's warehouse has now gone and in its place is a retail store. The Eagle Tavern sports a new inn sign, but you can't park outside it any more and there's limited parking on the opposite side - a descendant of the original Ford passes. Two traffic-calming humps have been created - one can be seen in the distance, at Corn Street corner.

ABINGDON: Though quiet when this picture was taken in 1976, the junction of Spring Road and Ock Street in Abingdon could be extremely busy. For one thing it was close to one of only two river bridges in the town, but more importantly it was only a matter of yards from the entrance of the MG car factory in Marcham Road. At the end of shifts, hundreds of MG workers - many on cycles - would pour from the factory gates, completely swamping any driver trying to travel in the opposite direction. *OPA*

The MG factory closed in 1980, but traffic in this part of Abingdon is still heavy at certain times of the day. To deal with this, the junction has a mini roundabout, metal barriers and a pelican crossing. The cottages in Ock Street on the right were recently demolished to be replaced by a development of apartments called Juniper Court. Note that among the roadsigns on the tall streetlight is one pointing to the MG Car Club. As MGs were made in the town for 51 years, it is entirely appropriate that the Club should now be based in Abingdon.

DIDCOT: This picture, taken in 1961 mid-way down the Broadway, shows Didcot's main shopping thoroughfare. Travelling along the Broadway is a Hillman car, and parked beside it can be identified a Commer van, a Vauxhall and a Bedford van. Station Road leads off to the left and at the junction there's a zebra crossing with flashing Belisha beacons. Incidentally, both *Woman's Realm* and *Radio Times*, advertised on the side-wall at the extreme left, are still going strong; *Radio Times* celebrated its 70th anniversary in 1993. *OPA*

A Pelican crossing has replaced the old-style one, and zigzag and double yellow lines stop vehicles parking at this spot. The roadsign on the right-hand side gives directions to Harwell village, and Oxford, Newbury and Wantage - a reminder that up until the 1930s Upper Broadway was known as Wantage or Harwell Road. Traffic humps have been recently installed along the wide, almost straight street in a bid to cut down on the high accident rate - there have been 34 accidents along the Broadway in the past five years.

WATLINGTON's narrow streets were lined with parked cars even in 1976. A one-way system round the Town Hall - from where this picture was taken - was needed to keep the cars and vans moving, as the 'No entry' road marking indicates. *OPA*

Parking on both sides of the High Street causes problems to traffic in modern-day Watlington too. Road markings have been changed in the intervening years, though a one-way system still operates. The 'No entry' marking has been obliterated, albeit none too neatly, and double white broken lines now give priority to the traffic in the High Street. Flower-tubs and Victorian-style streetlights have been added. Though the post office still survives, with the same twenty-year old sign above its door, the Hare and Hounds Hotel hasn't fared so well. It is presently up for sale as office space.

HENLEY-ON-THAMES: This is Hart Street as seen from the Market Place some time in the 1960s. About this time (1961-63) the Worboys Committee was appointed to review our traffic signs and make them easier to read. Looking at the confusing array of directions on this early example of a mini-roundabout, one can see why. Place names in capital letters were found to be difficult to read and a system using initial capitals and lower-case letters was introduced. Leading the line of traffic on the approach to the traffic lights is an MG Magnette with a Land-Rover and Ford Thames van not far behind. *OPA*

In the Hart Street of 1993 the buildings are largely untouched, though the road layout has been changed. This is still the meeting point of the roads to Reading, London and Oxford, and the traffic lights are still there, but the island and its many signs have gone. Instead, directional signs are positioned more usefully on the approaches to the junction, not when you get there. However, the grass strip down the centre of Hart Street has been removed.

The Highway Code

There are two books that people in Britain buy in huge quantities, then never read. One, of course, is the Bible. The other is the Highway Code. Since 1931, when the first edition was published, governments have been urging road users to refer regularly to their 'Bible of the Road', but to little avail. Most copies gather dust in the bottom of drawers.

More than 1.5 million people a year buy the Highway Code, usually when they are about to take their driving tests. But once the L-plates are off, most scarcely give another thought to stopping distances, arm signals or non-primary direction signs. In a survey carried out for Her Majesty's Stationery Office (which publishes the Highway Code), it was found that more than half the motorists questioned hadn't looked at the Highway Code for over three years.

Early editions were modest little things, scarcely more than leaflets. The 1947 version, for instance, had a dull brown cover and 32 pages of simple illustrations. But at only one (old) penny, it was good value and the text gives some interesting insights into postwar motoring conditions. In tone, it's a strange mixture of high morality and homely advice, as if it were written by a strict but sensible children's nanny. The Minister of Transport's foreword stresses the 'moral duty' of motorists to study and respect the Code. Elsewhere in the text, motorists are warned against driving 'in a spirit of competition' and exhorted to be 'courteous and kindly' and 'take a pride' in their driving.

Driving was a simpler pastime then. Traffic signs and signals, for instance, take up only two well-spaced pages in this edition; in contrast, the 1993 version has five closely printed pages on these subjects. The slower pace of life is reflected in the fact that stopping distances, printed inside the back cover of the post-war edition, only refer to speeds from 10 to 50 miles per hour, while today's Code goes from 20 to 70 mph. Some of it seems almost Dickensian with its section on horse-drawn vehicles and whip signals and its description of the good driver as 'master of his machine'. And nowhere in its pages does it acknowledge the existence of the woman driver.

By comparison, the 'fifties versions seem positively rakish. By 1959 the Code cost 6d, but for this you got colour and lively illustrations. Road

SIGNALS TO OTHER DRIVERS - *contd.*

Alternative signals which may be used by drivers of horse-drawn vehicles.

"I am going to STOP."

"I am going to TURN."

After rotating the whip, incline it to the right or left to show the direction in which the turn is to be made.

The 1947 Highway Code still showed whip signals.

signs now take up four pages, and not surprisingly the whip signals have been dropped. 1959 was the year Britain's first motorway, the M1, was opened, and for the first time a section on this new kind of driving appears. It includes an definition of exactly what a 'hard shoulder' is - '8 ft width of verge adjacent to the carriageway, strong enough to carry vehicles in an emergency' - and the first of many pleas to motorway drivers not to 'wander from lane to lane'.

The Codes published in the 'sixties reflect the changing conditions on the road. Photographs as well as diagrams and drawings are used to illustrate the everyday hazards of driving in more crowded conditions, such as children running into the road. More traffic means more traffic management, and innovations like 'pedestrian crossings controlled by push buttons', roundabout priorities and more complicated road markings had to be explained.

The cost and thickness of the Highway Codes continued to increase during the next decades. In 1978 it was up to 69 pages and cost 25p, and in 1987 74 pages for 60p. The complexities of driving were also on the increase. The carrying of dangerous goods and hints on the prevention of car theft appear for the first time. Even crossing

92. To reach a destination to the right of the motorway, you will leave by a slip road on your left. After leaving the motorway watch for signs directing you to the right via an underpass or a bridge.

93. If you miss your exit, continue along the carriageway until the next exit.

94. When you leave the motorway, remember to adjust your driving to the different conditions of the ordinary road system.

The 1959 instructions on leaving the motorway.

the road became more complicated. Instead of the simple kerb drill of 'Stop, look right, left and right again', parents were urged to teach their children the much longer Green Cross Code.

The latest edition of the Code, the first major update for 15 years, was issued in 1993 at 99p. Though it might have 76 bright and brash pages full of important information on car telephones, tactile paving and Puffin crossings, in some ways it harks back to its little brown 1947 predecessor. Having speeded up the traffic by building motorways and bypasses, we're now slowing it down to postwar levels with man-made obstructions. Cyclists in particular are told to 'take care near road humps, narrowings and other traffic calming features.' And the horses are back. No less than nine paragraphs are addressed to horse-riders; modern riders using the roads, for instance, are advised to 'avoid roundabouts wherever possible'. Like all Highway Codes, this new version is packed with good advice, but how many of us will read it?

All illustrations from the Highway Code: Crown Copyright, reproduced with the permission of the Controller of Her Majesty's Stationery Office

59 Be careful near a parked ice-cream van — children are more interested in ice-cream than in traffic.

60 When coming to a Zebra crossing, keep a look out for pedestrians waiting to cross (particularly children, the elderly, the infirm and people with prams) and be ready to slow down or stop to let them cross. When anyone has stepped on to a crossing, you must give way. Signal to other drivers that you mean to slow down or stop. Allow more time for stopping on wet or icy roads. Do not signal pedestrians to cross; another vehicle may be approaching.

16

Real-life situations are illustrated in 1987.

The modern cyclist: a page from the latest 1993 Highway Code.

189. Fit a bell and use it when necessary to warn other road users, particularly blind and partially sighted pedestrians, that you are there.

Wear clothes which will help you to be seen.

SAFETY EQUIPMENT AND CLOTHING

190. Wear a cycle helmet which conforms to recognised safety standards. Choose appropriate clothes for cycling. Avoid long coats or other clothes which may get tangled in the chain or a wheel. Light-coloured or fluorescent clothing helps other road users see you in daylight and poor visibility.

191. At night you **MUST** use front and rear lights and a red rear reflector. Reflective material such as belts, arm and ankle bands, wheel reflectors and 'spacer' flags will also help you to be seen at night.

6. Time has passed them by

LOCKINGE: No, a Victorian snapshot hasn't slipped in by accident. This is not the turn of the century, it's 28 June 1956 and Ken Cook is delivering milk by horse and cart in the estate village of Lockinge. His deliveries were to continue for only a year or two more, before this picturesque anachronism came to an end. The harmony of the scene is not accidental - the whole village of Lockinge, including the roads, cottages and other buildings, was designed and built in the 1860s by the landowner, Lord Wantage. To the right of the milk-cart is the postbox, set into the wall outside the post office. *OPA*

Though it's still an idyllic scene in 1993, there have been a few changes. The narrow walled lane is untouched by time, but the cottages on the right were demolished in the early 1960s to create parking spaces for cars - the need for private car parking was one thing that Lord Wantage didn't foresee. There have been some tree losses too: all the Scots pines have gone and one or two elms were lost in the interim, but the limes on the left have survived and the manicured yews lining the lane look even smarter. A sign on the verge reminds visitors that this is not a through road to the Downs.

CHARLBURY: When this picture of Church Street in Charlbury was taken in 1968, there was some concern over its conservation. A survey of the village sponsored by the Council for the Protection of Rural England wanted the street and all its buildings preserved for their group value. Looking at it, one can appreciate why. Outside the one remaining shop in the street is a favourite of the 'sixties, a little Minivan, and close to it a Humber. *OPA*

Well, the CPRE got their wish and the street retains its Cotswold charm some 25 years later. Charlbury hasn't completely avoided moving with the times, however. 'No parking' signs and double yellow lines have crept in and, where permitted, motorists take full advantage of the parking. There's also been some tidying up of the kerb edges. As for the buildings, another village shop has closed and been turned into a private house. In place of the Minivan, ascending the gentle slope of Church Street is a modern all-purpose country vehicle, the Range Rover.

Ducklington.

DUCKLINGTON village pond in the 1960s presents a lovely rural picture. The ancient church overlooks the pond and the war memorial, and surrounding the green are pretty cottages. An early roadsign, possibly dating back to the immediate postwar period, points to Aston and Bampton along an unclassified road and to Witney and Oxford, Standlake and Abingdon along the A415. The only fly in the ointment - the pond seems to have completely dried out. *OPA*

Today's pond is definitely wet, as the reeds prove. The cluster of roadsigns and the intrusive electricity pole and streetlight on the left do not enhance the contemporary scene. The roadsign uses the so-called 'transport alphabet' devised by Jock Kinnear in 1967. But on the plus side, on this day, 23 March 1993, there was a carpet of daffodils, as well as a new wooden bench from which to admire them.

EYNSHAM: This is the Square at the heart of Eynsham, as it looked in December 1975, complete with a parked American car - possibly a Chevrolet - and what looks like one of the first Japanese imported motorbikes. Through the gap in the buildings can be seen the High Street. On the left, surrounded by railings, is the rather battered original village cross, with the 19th-century metal 'corset' that held it together. The building on the right is the Bartholomew Room, erstwhile prison and market hall. It was bought in 1977 for the people of Eynsham as a community building. *OPA*

The same scene in 1993, with a car parked in almost exactly the same place. The uncorseted cross is a replacement, carved and erected in February 1991, though it is surrounded by the original 19th-century railings. The renovated Bartholomew Room's forbidding appearance is softened by tubs of flowers and, in the summer, window-boxes.

SUTTON COURTENAY: Church Street in 1948, and behind the hedge lurks a row of four motor cars. So many cars in one village, so soon after the end of the war, was quite an unusual sight and is indicative of a prosperous gathering. The poor old motorist was very hard hit at this time. Strict petrol rationing was still in operation and the basic ration for private motoring only gave enough fuel to travel about 100 miles a month. This situation continued until June 1950, when petrol rationing was ended. *BR/OPC Collection*

In April 1993 the village scene is still easy on the eye, though it has been brought up to date a little. The road has been widened, its edges tidied up and white lines painted. Cottage-owners, as well as families living in the 'big house', are now car-owners, and some of them have converted their front gardens into off-street parking places.

SHENINGTON: Some time in the 1960s this Austin Somerset was caught by the camera in the village of Shenington in the north of the county. One of the old-style red public telephone boxes is beside the road. In the shade of the tree stand the milk churns from a local farm, a common rural sight in those days before milk tankers. *OPA*

This is the same road junction more than thirty years later. There have been some changes: the benches have been replaced and moved, road markings and a bus shelter have been added, and a new BT telephone box has replaced the old one. Why is it that these new-style boxes stick out like sore thumbs in such traditional settings? Perhaps even more striking are the changes to the buildings: the one on the left has been reduced by a storey, and the cottage in the background is now only half thatched.

On the road with the RAC

The RAC has offered emergency roadside assistance to motorists since its earliest days. Founded as the Automobile Club of Great Britain and Ireland in 1897, it was Britain's first motoring organisation. It took its present title in 1907, and at first help was given via a nationwide network of touring guides, working as a sort of back-up service to the police. Later road patrols were set up, with patrolmen cruising main and secondary roads on motor-cycle combinations, on the look-out for motorists in trouble.

For a short time in the 1960s there was a special patrol force of women, called 'patrolettes', who travelled around on motor scooters - female 'Knights of the Road' are few and far between today, however. As an equal opportunities employer, the RAC say they would like to employ more women as service patrols, but in practice they find that there are disappointingly few well-qualified woman mechanics who are interested in the job.

Whatever form the patrol service takes, one of its most important needs is communication, which was why roadside telephone boxes came into being. They were primarily for use by patrol officers, keeping them in touch with their local base and acting like a mini-office, but of course they were also available day and night for motorists to summon help. Though they are rival organisations, over the years the RAC and AA have co-operated remarkably well with each other in providing reciprocal emergency arrangements for members, on the sound principle that one should never abandon stranded drivers, no matter to which motoring organisation they belong.

The first RAC roadside box was installed in 1919, in Egham in Surrey, and by 1947 the number had grown to 550. Paradoxically, though the RAC now has a membership of 5.6 million

Left A 1960s RAC 'patrolette', complete with Vespa.

Below A wooden RAC box, pictured in 1954 on the A40 London to Oxford road, at Stokenchurch, Buckinghamshire.

The RAC stand at the Royal Agricultural Show, held at Oxford in 1959.

motorists, there are fewer RAC boxes today - 470 at the last count. This is because patrol officers now keep in touch using an in-car communications system and motorway routes are equipped with their own independent emergency telephone system, leaving the motoring organisations to cater for trunk routes and more remote areas. And, of course, some drivers have their own car telephones.

The wooden RAC boxes of the 1950s, with stable door openings, have all disappeared, but they are still remembered fondly by the patrols and motorists who used them. Each member had his or her own key for the lock, and RAC and AA boxes had identical locks, so boxes could be used by members of either organisation. Inside there was a wooden shelf and a black telephone for speaking to the local office and, if you were lucky, in those more trusting times you might find emergency supplies of fuel and water.

In the 1960s roadside services for members were extended. When the RAC visited the Royal Agricultural Show at Oxford in 1959, they were able to show off a fine collection of their vehicles. As well as a mobile office there was a Norton motor-cycle combination, used by RAC patrols until 1965, and an RAC Land-Rover, now replaced by various four-wheel-drive vehicles.

It was at about this time too that the appearance of the boxes changed rapidly and fibreglass began to replace wood. In the early days these boxes had STD payphones, but later came so-called 'mono call' telephones, connected to the local RAC office. At the same time some continental call boxes were introduced, much more like the emergency phones we are used to seeing today. Again, the motorist had simply to press a button and the local RAC number was dialled automatically.

Modern emergency call boxes of the 1990s are self-dialling, operating 'hands-free', with speakers in the wings and a built-in microphone. Whereas in the past they were connected to a local command centre, since the mid-1980s they have been channelled through a national computer system. All very high-tech and efficient, but on a windswept night perhaps not quite as inviting as a cosy wooden RAC box.

A fibreglass box in use at Heathrow Airport in August 1966.

The caption to this 1960s publicity shot reads 'a motorist and his wife phone for help from one of the new continental-type telephone boxes which the RAC are erecting'.

All photographs courtesy of The Library, The Royal Automobile Club

7. Bridges

SWINFORD TOLL BRIDGE: Two questions are posed by this photograph taken during the 1960s of the toll bridge over the Thames on the B4044 near Eynsham. Who is the VIP in the Austin Princess, and did the official or the saluting policeman have the nerve to demand a toll payment from him or her? The bridge was built under Act of Parliament for the 4th Earl of Abingdon in 1767 and is one of two in the county that still demand tolls - the other is at Whitchurch. Despite being described in 1905 as 'an anachronism', Swinford Toll Bridge still operates. *OPA*

The toll bridge as it looks today, still charging its 2p levy and crossed by up to 15,000 vehicles daily. Since the 'sixties the gate has been removed, a traffic island has been created in the middle of the road and an ugly but functional plastic waterproof shelter provided for the toll gatherers.

Left As the sign explains, the present toll for 'private motor cars' is 2p. There have been recent attempts to increase the charge: in 1983 to 10p and in 1993 to 5p. The current owners say they need the extra income for some urgent bridge repairs. But motorists are not keen to 'stand and deliver' and proposals to raise the charge inevitably lead to a public outcry. However, far from dying out, road tolls might become more widespread in the future. Charging a premium to use the motorways is one idea the government is considering to help fund road improvements, though we are unlikely to see motorway toll booths. Other methods, like annual permits or an electronic tagging system, are being looked at.

WHITCHURCH-ON-THAMES is the home of Oxfordshire's other toll bridge. The first toll bridge was built here in 1793, replacing the earlier ferry service, remembered in the name of a nearby pub, the Ferry Boat Inn. The present iron bridge dates back to Victorian times and only qualifies as an Oxfordshire landmark by a matter of yards, since it stands right on the Oxfordshire/Berkshire border, with the county boundary on the Pangbourne side. This is how it looked around 1947, from the Berkshire bank. *Postcard (Bridge House Real Photo Series) from Peter Woodage collection*

From a distance, the bridge today looks unchanged from the 'forties, though in the meantime the road has been resurfaced and the bridge's metal supports inspected by divers from time to time for signs of decay. Under the bridge to the right is Whitchurch lock, kept busy these days by the frequent passage of pleasure craft. Pangbourne Meadow, from where this was taken, provides an attractive mooring for people enjoying a boating holiday on the Thames.

For many years, those collecting the tolls sheltered in the porch of the toll-house (seen here on the right) and simply stepped out into the road as vehicles passed. That was all changed in the spring of 1993, when modern additions were made to the bridge to make the collecting of tolls easier. Road humps slow the traffic and a brick toll booth with two swing barriers has been erected on the Oxfordshire side - quite a 'Check Point Charlie' in fact. The present charge for cars is 6p, though as at Swinford there have been recent applications to up the toll. In my experience it's not so much the amount of the tolls that people object to, it's the delays caused by their collection.

WALLINGFORD: This Bedford van and ARC lorry just manage to squeeze past each other on Wallingford Bridge in January 1974, while a pedestrian struggles up the narrow path in the wind and the rain. This bridge over the Thames, part of which dates from medieval times, was clearly having difficulty coping with the volume of heavy traffic passing over it at this time. *OPA*

The wear and tear on both bridge and pedestrians has been alleviated by February 1993. After trying various systems for coping with the traffic, the present arrangement was settled on: traffic lights allow only one line of vehicles to cross at a time, and the footpath has been widened so there's room for two pedestrians to walk abreast. The bridge lights are interesting; in 1981 they were replaced by new ones, cast by a local iron-founder from moulds taken from the originals. The pedestals and columns are now topped by lanterns decorated with finials and domes, much more in keeping with the period style than the lanterns of the 'seventies. The unusual spire glimpsed through the trees on the left belongs to St Peter's Church; though still a consecrated building, it is now a redundant church.

CULHAM: There are no fewer than five bridges in or near Culham, not a bad record for a small village. Seen here is Sutton Courtenay Bridge, a listed structure with three arches that has suffered at the hands of the 20th century. Grouped with it, carrying Tollgate Road past the lock and spanning the River Thames and Culham Cut, are Culham Cut Bridge and a small two-arched bridge at present running over a dry bed. To add to the motoring hazards at this point there is also a double bend, which this Rover is in the process of negotiating. Small wonder then that the bridges here show many signs of scrapes and bumps. Pedestrians had their work cut out too at this time (1975), with such a narrow pavement. Out of interest, the other two bridges are on the western edge of the village: one carries the A415 road, and close to it is Culham Old Bridge, now closed to traffic but complete with a tollgate cottage. *OPA*

It's February 1993 and the bridges at Culham show even more signs of wear and tear, and continue to carry two-way traffic, including lorries. Handrails and parapets have been damaged and repaired several times after arguments with various vehicles, but at least the pathway for walkers and anglers has been widened and improved. You would think that no one in their right mind would even consider parking on such a hazardous stretch of road, but no doubt, without the double yellow lines and prominent 'No parking at any time' signs, someone would pause in their car on the brow of the bridge to enjoy the view.

COWLEY: A local landmark, this 25-metre conveyor bridge, pictured in 1967, passed over Oxford's Eastern Bypass close to the Watlington Road roundabout. It was erected in the 1960s and during its thirty-year lifetime ferried millions of cars from the body plant at Cowley, on the left, across the bypass to the assembly factories at North and South Works. *OPA*

Rover's car manufacturing processes are now concentrated on production lines on one side of the bypass and the bridge is no longer needed. The North and South Works are surplus to requirements too; they were closed in 1992 and the site is being developed as a new business park and hotel. This was the scene on 28 May 1993, with demolition work of the buildings well under way and the bridge partially demolished. The crane on the right is lifting away parts of the bridge.

Watched by many ex-Cowley workers, the main span of the bridge was taken down on 30 May 1993, bringing a part of Oxford's industrial history to an end. A stretch of the bypass was closed to traffic for the day and a giant 500-tonne crane was used to lift the steel bridge from its position and lower it on to the ground in North Works, where it was broken up and recycled. This is how it looked on 2 June, with the bridge gone, the North and South Works sites being cleared and scaffolding being put up on the twin chimneys, so that they in their turn can be dismantled brick by brick.

8. Bypassed at last

BOTLEY: The makeshift sign propped against a road-sign in West Way, Botley (see also page28), almost begs for the addition of at least one exclamation mark. It's someone's rather low-key way of announcing the opening of the A420 Cumnor Hill Bypass in August 1977, a fact that the roadsign doesn't reflect. It still directs traffic for Swindon and Bristol straight on through Botley and Cumnor Hill, rather than right on to the new bypass. Just visible beneath the main roadsign is one with a white background, indicating a non-primary route, pointing left to the village of North Hinksey. *OPA*

All three signs have changed since August 1977. The directional sign is now black-on-white and all through traffic is directed right for the ring road and the A420. The North Hinksey sign has been moved further down the road and the triumphant 'By-pass open' board has been superseded by one advertising pub food. When the bypass was built, it was hoped that Oxford's ring road would go a long way to solving the city's traffic problems. This proved not to be the case because in the main the congestion was caused by local, not long-distance, traffic.

BOTLEY: A real trip down Memory Lane - back in August 1955, before the Cumnor Hill Bypass was even a twinkle in anyone's eye, the B4044 Eynsham Road out of Botley looked like this. Just another quiet single-lane country road, with overgrown grass verges. *OPA*

There's no gain without pain, they say, and in this case it's certainly true. The lane is gone forever. Widened, with a footpath, roadsigns, streetlights and kerbstones, it now carries a much heavier load of traffic north-west to Eynsham and Witney, while above it rumbles the almost constant traffic of the A420 Cumnor Hill Bypass.

Above DORCHESTER-ON-THAMES: More than four decades separate the first picture from the last. In June 1949, the General Post Office van collects the afternoon mail from an almost deserted High Street. Next to the post office is the black and white frontage of Weavers Cottage, which has served as a post office and sorting office in the past. Opposite, the 16th-century George Hotel stands as a landmark. Note the inn signs - both show St George, the dragon-killer, though for a time in the 1980s the sign depicted King George III. During wartime, the GPO accepted almost any vehicle available to it, but after the war it went back to using mainly Morris Commercial vans, which this appears to be. *Crown Copyright*

Above right In the 1960s an estimated 20,000 vehicles a day thundered through the village, which lay on the main A423 route from Oxford to Henley. It was said that some elderly villagers hadn't dare cross the road for many years. Villagers campaigned long and hard

for a bypass to be built, and on 5 November 1982 they got their wish when it was finally opened. Now renumbered A4074, it passes to the north-east of the village, is 1.6 miles long and includes a new bridge over the River Thame to relieve the stone Dorchester Bridge (1813-1815). *Crown Copyright, reproduced with permission of Controller, HMSO*

Right In recent years this view of Dorchester's High Street was considered beautiful enough to feature in the film adaptation of E. M. Forster's *Howard's End*. Certainly heavy through traffic is no longer a problem, but parked cars and vans along the High Street are. Far from feeling 'cut off' now the bypass has been built, locals say that they get more visitors than ever to their famous 12th-century Abbey. Notice that since the postwar picture, the post office has moved to premises next door, and today's red Royal Mail van is a Freight Rover Sherpa Di diesel.

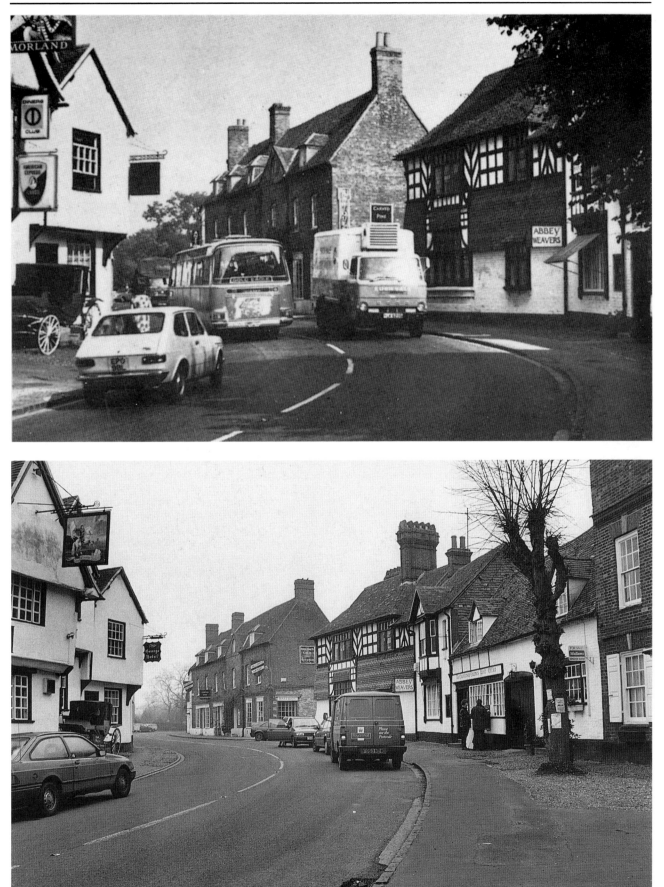

FARINGDON: The campaign for a bypass round the market town of Faringdon was another long-fought and sometimes ill-tempered battle, as this scene with demonstrators sitting down in front of a Bedford truck in December 1972 shows. In spite of public pressure and national publicity, inhabitants and traders had to wait another seven years before the bypass was finally opened in 12 July 1979. *OPA*

The second photograph, taken in 1979, clearly shows what Faringdon had to put up with prior to the opening of its bypass (see also page 10). Narrow London Street is clogged with traffic, much of it lorries, and traffic lights were needed. Heavy lorries passing up the hill in that confined space caused frequent jams as well as damage to buildings.

The scene today is altogether more tranquil. There is no longer a need for traffic lights and pedestrians can cross the Market Place in safety. A 'Buses only' area has been marked out in the centre beside the Town Hall. But not all the effects of the bypass were beneficial, as other towns and villages have found. When the traffic vanished from the narrow streets of Faringdon, so did the tourists. Shops and pubs, such as the Bell pictured here, found that they had lost much of their passing trade. In 1985 permission was given by the Department of Transport for the erection of specially made experimental tourist signboards on the A420 - the first of their kind in the country. This was followed in 1986 by permanent white on brown signs, drawing motorists' attention to the 'historic market town'.

DRAYTON: At this time in 1965 the A34 Oxford to Newbury road passed right through the centre of the village of Drayton. To add to the problems faced by the village schoolchildren, for a time the primary school operated on a split site on either side of the very busy trunk road. This made the services of the school crossing patrol officer, or 'lollipop lady', pictured here on 9 July 1965, even more of a necessity than usual. The design of the 'lollipop' itself has changed since the 'sixties: a red-bordered round yellow sign now bears the words 'STOP - CHILDREN' and a black bar. *OPA*

The same junction today, and traffic through the village has greatly decreased since the opening of the A34 Abingdon Bypass in October 1973 and the downgrading of this road to the B4017. Drayton School is now on one site so there is no longer need for a school crossing patrol, or a zebra crossing here; instead there is a mini-roundabout. Streetlighting has been increased and there is a new road sign. Also, in the intervening years the mature tree, seen on the right in 1965, seems to have fallen victim to old age or disease, but the ivy beside the Wheatsheaf pub has all but obliterated the electricity pole.

OLD WOODSTOCK: This is Manor Road, showing Bedford and Leyland lorries descending the hill in the 1980s. At this time the road (then the A34) was the trunk road to and from the Midlands and was heavily congested, with Woodstock and other towns along the route suffering the consequences. *OPA*

This is the scene today. Though not strictly bypassed, since the opening of the M40 extension Woodstock has been relieved of some of its heaviest traffic - some say the amount of traffic on the Oxford to Stratford part of the route (now the A44) has been halved. However, the route is still well used and there are calls for a Woodstock bypass.

Abingdon and the Midget

MGs have often been called 'the world's favourite sports car', and of all MGs none is looked on more fondly than the Midget. For more than fifty years from 1929 until 1980, the Midget, along with other marques and models, was produced in Abingdon. Given the enduring affection which exists worldwide for the company and its undoubted commercial success, is it any wonder that many people still mourn its passing?

At one time the Marcham Road factory was the biggest sports car factory in the world and, in all, more than a million sports cars came out of its gates, three-quarters of them destined for export. For much of that time, mechanisation of the factory was minimal: vehicles were pushed manually along the line and until 1975 every machine was individually road tested. Not only MGs were made at Abingdon; over the years Rileys, Morris Minor vans and Travellers and Austin-Healey Sprites were also produced there, as well as competition cars like the Mini-Cooper.

The history of MG started in 1922, as an offshoot of William Morris's Oxford car-making empire. The sports cars were the brainchild of Cecil Kimber, manager of the Morris Garages - the initials gave him the inspiration for the company name and the design of the famous octagonal MG logo.

The first Midget was the M-type, which saw the light of day at the London Motor Show a year before MG's move to Abingdon. It was based on the 847cc four-cylinder Morris Minor engine, and was an immediate success. Its appeal was the same as that of all Midgets over the decades: it looked and handled like a sports car, but it was within the means of most ordinary drivers. Enthusiasts talk of the thrilling sensation of speed and responsiveness as they zip round corners. In other words, Midgets are affordable motoring fun.

A succession of four-cylinder models followed the M-type, including the J2 and the famous EX127 record-breaking racing model of the 'thirties. Known affectionately as the Magic Midget, the EX127 is immortalised in Abingdon in a pub name and sign.

The outbreak of the Second World War brought car production in Abingdon to a temporary halt in favour of armament work, most notably the production of the main section of the Albemarle

The plaque on the wall of the Boundary House, a Morland public house in Abingdon, honouring Cecil Kimber, whose home this used to be. The plaque was placed there by the MGT New England Club of America. Morland's association with MG goes further - a beer was brewed to mark the 50th anniversary of the factory's coming to Abingdon and was called Old Speckled Hen, after a one-off 14/40 model MG car of 1929, which had unusual black and gold flecked paintwork. *Author*

The sign outside the Magic Midget pub in Midget Close, Abingdon, another Morland house, commemorating the EX127's achievement of reaching 120.56 mph in 1932. The pub bars are called Brooklands and Pendine and there are also two murals on the exterior walls depicting the Magic Midget in action. *Author*

The TC production line at Abingdon in around 1948. On the left is the Y-type production line. *BMIHT/Rover Group*

bomber and the assembly of Rolls-Royce Merlin engines for Lancasters and Spitfires. But within weeks of the war ending, production of the T-series Midget, which had begun in the 1930s, started up again. Of the 1,500 TCs built in 1946, more than a third were for the overseas market. Including purchase tax, the price in 1946 was £528.

American servicemen posted here were particularly taken by this model, and when they returned home many shipped their TCs after them. This proved to be the beginning of a long love affair between America and the Abingdon sports car. The little two-seater was well-loved at home too: the Duke of Edinburgh, then a young naval officer, often took his girlfriend Princess Elizabeth out for a spin in his new TC.

Late in 1949 a redesigned TD model followed, the first Midget to have the luxury of bumpers front and rear. Initially it was well received, especially overseas, but soon began to look decidedly old-fashioned. An updated TF was launched in 1953, but never really caught on, especially in the face of competition from the Triumph TR2. By the mid-'fifties it was clear that a total rethink of design was urgently needed. This brainstorming led to the creation of a sports car like no other MG had ever produced, the MGA. Gone were the familiar huge mudguards and the square body - in their place was a racy, streamlined tourer capable of a top speed close on 100 mph.

This was a boom time for MG, by then part of the British Motor Corporation, culminating in the launch in 1962 of the MGB, ultimately the best-selling MG of all. Of the half a million MGBs and MGB GT coupés manufactured between 1962 and 1980, 390,000 were exported, mainly - naturally - to the United States.

So great was the success of the MGA and later the MGB that the lovable Midget was overshadowed for a time. But in 1961 it made its comeback in the shape of a new baby sports car known simply as the MG Midget. This was produced alongside the Austin-Healey Sprite, and collectively these two became known by enthusiasts as 'Spridgets'.

It was a bone of contention between owners of the rival Abingdon sports cars that the Sprite was consistently priced slightly lower than the Midget - in 1962 the difference was £27. 'Spridgets' stayed in production for two decades, much of

A 1968 MG Midget Mk III. *David Frost*

their popularity coming from the fact that they were different and exciting at a time when cars were becoming bland and similar.

The 1970s brought a huge increase in the price of fuel, stringent new safety requirements in the North American car market, and British economic policies that caused the pound to rise steeply against the dollar. All these factors hit the sports car export market very hard. Though MG managed to weather the crises, and the MGB and Midget continued to be built, this was to be the beginning of the end. In 1980, less than a year after the whole of Abingdon joined with the workforce in celebrating the company's half century in the town, British Leyland decided to pull the plug. And despite last-minute attempts to save it, the factory gates shut for the last time on 24 October 1980.

But the story doesn't quite end there. More than a decade after the Abingdon factory closed and production ceased, enthusiasm for its cars is

A 1980 Midget 1500, one of the last of the line. *Chris Hill*

launched to create the first MG museum at Abingdon.

You can still encounter lovingly restored MG classics and well-used MG workhorses on British and foreign roads. And the name itself has never really died. Rover revived it in the late 1980s and gave it to sporty versions of the Metro, Maestro and Montego saloon ranges in a process known as badge-engineering.

But the 1990s have seen the Phoenix truly rise again. The first MG sports car in thirteen years, a £25,000 special edition roadster, is currently in production at Cowley. Called the MG RV8, it's being built to commemorate the 30th anniversary of the first MGB. And, more than that, Rover is making plans to produce a new affordable small sports car by the middle of the decade, a worthy successor to the much-missed Midget.

undiminished. The MG Car Club, founded in 1930, is still a thriving world-wide organisation with members as far afield as Hawaii and Tasmania. Since April 1992 it has been housed in a building next door to the old MG Administration Block in Cemetery Road, Abingdon. A separate appeal has also been

The MG RV8, currently being hand-built at Cowley. *Rover Cars*

9. Gone but not forgotten

ABINGDON: On 18 November 1980, just over three weeks after it closed for the last time, this was the scene at Gate 3 of the MG factory. On the right you can see the famous octagon and the company flag still flying bravely. The MG Car Company moved to the Marcham Road site in 1929 and stayed for 51 years, in that time producing more than a million sports cars, 75 per cent of them for export to America. A Block, facing Marcham Road on the right of the picture, housed the main assembly complex. (See the preceding feature on Abingdon and the Midget.) *OPA*

On 11 February 1993 all remnants of Gate 3 are long gone. In its place is a roundabout, coping with traffic generated by Abingdon Business Park and the nearby trading estate at Nuffield Way, named of course after Lord Nuffield, William Morris. Though some of the original MG buildings were demolished to make way for the Business Park, the sloping roofs of A Block, now reclad, are clearly recognisable in this picture. The decorative gable, which once carried the octagon logo, is still there too. B Block, which housed operations such as tyre-fitting, despatch, design and development, and finishing, is also still standing, though not shown here.

BANBURY: These cars in Parsons Street some time in the 1950s, one of them a Morris 8, are waiting outside Brown's Original Cake Shop. Forty years ago, in Banbury and in other towns, it was still possible to nip into town and be reasonably sure of a parking space right outside the shops - if, that is, you were lucky enough to own a car. The Original Cake Shop was started on this site in the 18th century by Betty and Jarvis White, and the famous Banbury cakes were sold here right up until 1968, when the building was demolished. *OPA*

Today narrow Parsons Street on a weekday is choked with delivery vehicles. As for Brown's, it is only thanks to Ye Olde Reine Deer Inn sign, which still overhangs the street, that it's possible to locate its site. Instead of the cake shop there is now a characterless red-brick building. But all is not lost - 'Genuine Banbury cakes' are still advertised for sale across the street in a tea shop in one of the town's original Tudor buildings.

DIDCOT: Until its railway station was opened in 1844 as part of Brunel's Great Western Railway, Didcot was just another remote and insignificant village. When this photograph of the station forecourt was taken in 1962, it still had a rural air. The roundabout, known as the Station Mound, was thought to have been created from earth dug out when the tunnels under the station were built. In 1961 the Great Western Society was formed to collect and preserve examples from the golden age of steam. It still has its home at Didcot Station and runs the Didcot Railway Centre, a working museum of mostly GWR steam locomotives and rolling-stock. *OPA*

By January 1993 all that remains of the Station Mound is a narrow grass strip. Most of the trees went in the early 1970s, though the line of poplars has survived. In 1985 the railway station was given a complete facelift and its name changed to Didcot Parkway. The forecourt has parking for taxis only, but there

is space for 1,510 cars in the huge car park over the station footbridge, catering mainly for the several thousand commuters who travel daily from Didcot to Paddington. In the background are the cooling towers of Didcot Power Station, commissioned in 1970.

CHIPPING NORTON: This narrow junction is where Chipping Norton High Street meets Burford Road and West Street, as it looked in 1957. An old Oxford County 'Polo mint'-style signpost points to Charlbury and Witney along the A361. Some of these signs can still be seen standing beside out-of-the-way Oxfordshire roads. An advertisement for popular cigarettes of the time, Wills's Gold Flake, is displayed on the wall of the row of terraced cottages. Gold Flake cigarettes have a very long history, the brand having been on sale for more than a century, from 1883 to 1988. Gold Flake tobacco was around for almost as long, from 1897 until 1965. *OPA*

If it were not for the landmark of the King's Arms, the junction would be unrecognisable in 1993. Some of the cottages have gone in order for the road to be widened. In place of the old three-way junction there is now a mini-roundabout, and a public call box has been installed on the new open space. And what do you almost always get when you have open spaces in town centres these days? That's right, bollards.

10. Caution - roadworks

ENSTONE: An emergency situation on the A34 at Enstone on 24 February 1967. The wall of the house beside the main road is collapsing and has had to be shored up with planks. It's not clear whether this was due to the vibration of the traffic passing by, a collision or just old age. While work is going on, a workman operates stop-go signals, signalling to the waiting Sprite and Triumph Herald behind that they can pass. *OPA*

The road (now the A44) is marked with double white lines at this point, as it climbs the hill into Enstone. The houses on the right-hand side have survived the last quarter of a century remarkably well. But, alas, no coffee - or any other drink - is served at the Litchfield Arms Hotel. It was knocked down in 1974 and no physical trace of it is left, but its name lingers on in the new housing development built in its place, called Litchfield Close.

CHIPPING NORTON: When it was decided to widen the junction of New Street and High Street, the Corner Cafe building just had to go. This is the scene on 24 May 1969 as demolition work began. Wooden barriers cordon off the site and police officers are directing the traffic and keeping curious onlookers away. These days officers on traffic duty would wear reflective caps and jackets, rather than helmets and armbands. *OPA*

This is how it looked when the building was finally demolished, with New Street totally blocked by builders' vehicles and debris, and a workman on traffic duty. The roadsign on the corner of the white building directs motorists to Broadway, Worcester, Moreton and Stow. *OPA*

The same junction as it is today, with a pelican crossing and several new buildings to the right. The road opposite New Street has been blocked off with bollards and the space now provides extra car parking. Yet more bollards, this time concrete, prevent anyone parking on the pavement.

DIDCOT LINK ROAD: A busy scene looking east-wards during the construction of the A4130 link road joining Didcot to the A34, the Midlands to South Coast road. Site workers' cars seen here include a Triumph Dolomite and a Hillman Avenger. The link road passes close by Didcot Power Station which was built by the CEGB between 1965 and September 1970. The huge cooling towers can be seen for many miles and act as useful landmarks for those drivers whose sense of direction is shaky. It's no wonder it can be seen from afar - the six cooling towers are 114 m (275 feet) high, big enough for each one to contain St Paul's Cathedral.
OPA

The link road, seen on a misty October day in 1992 from a lower perspective, is now very much in use. Much of its traffic goes to and from Didcot Parkway Station, the nearby industrial estate at Milton Park or the scientific laboratories at Harwell and Chilton. Just visible on the right-hand side is a Mobil petrol station, built in the 1980s.

BURFORD: The roundabout at the busy crossroads of the A40 and the A361, just outside Burford, was constructed in 1967. When this photograph was taken, a Triumph Herald and a Morris Minor van were negotiating the
newly opened roundabout. On the right is the aptly named Cotswold Gateway Hotel. *OPA*

In 1993 the Peugeot on the right waits patiently for its turn to enter the roundabout. Today we take this sort of
scene for granted, but until 1966 there were no rules governing priority on roundabouts. Drivers were simply
expected to merge into the existing traffic. This worked well when there were fewer cars on the roads, but as the
volume of traffic increased it was decided to introduce the general rule that vehicles entering a roundabout should
give way to vehicles already on it. As can be seen in this picture, there are no signs to instruct approaching drivers
to give way, except the broken white lines on the road.

THAME: What's going on here? Your guess is as good as mine. The caption to this 1959 picture says that it shows a 'bridge to carry water for filling hole left by gas holder'. Was it an attempt to create an artificial lake, perhaps? Certainly water is being diverted over the Aylesbury Road via flexible pipes attached to each end of the metal frame. At this time it was quiet enough for a man to stand in the middle of the road and chat to his friend driving the Vauxhall.

'Cat's-eyes' - or reflecting road studs, to give them their proper name - run up the centre white line of the road. They were invented in 1934 by Percy Shaw of Halifax, who was inspired by seeing how the light reflected from tramlines at night. They began to be introduced in the later 'thirties and by this time were widespread. *OPA*

In 1993 it's not so easy to snatch a picture while dodging the traffic on the Aylesbury Road, even though Thame now has a bypass. Over the decades the cat's-eyes have gone, some of the power lines have been removed, and streetlights have been installed. There's no sign of a lake.

Double take!

Not really nostalgia, but worth including for the entertainment value! Roadsigns serve many useful functions, reminding us of the regulations, telling us how fast or slow to travel, warning us of hazards or directing us safely on our way. But just occasionally you come across a roadsign that makes you smile, one that tempts you to turn round (when it's safe to do so, of course), drive back and take another look. Did that sign really say what I thought it said?

Above Look out, webbed feet on the street! A similar triangular warning sign exists to protect wildfowl. In this case it is ducks who persist in wandering into the road. It really isn't their fault, as at this point a brook flows very close to the trunk road, and there's a nasty bend too. How effective these signs are is a moot point: when this photograph was taken a pathetic pile of flattened feathers lay in the road, suggesting that some drivers don't take them too seriously.

Above Beware, toads on roads! This is an authorised Department of Transport sign, designed to help prevent sex-mad toads being squashed on the roads as they head for their spawning ponds in the spring, oblivious of the traffic. Toad signs are put up from January onwards and have to be taken down by the end of May. At the last count there were 453 authorised toad-crossing sites in Britain (eight of them in Oxfordshire). All of them are registered with Herpetofauna Conservation International, who act for the DOT, collecting information and assessing the sites. They also organise toad patrols, toad fences and tunnels to help these creatures.

Right Is this someone's cruel idea of a joke? If it *is* an emergency, those will be twenty very long miles indeed! Ever since the M40 opened in 1991, red-faced, cross-legged motorists have complained about its lack of facilities. Not only were there no toilets along the motorway, but nowhere to eat or buy petrol either. In fact, drivers could travel 155 miles from Dover to Birmingham without seeing any motorway services. The situation was slightly improved after these temporary facilities were set up just off Junction 10. More permanent relief is in sight, however. At the time of writing, a £20 million service area is under construction at Ardley and due to be in use early in 1994.

Above How on earth did this perfectly ordinary street in the village of Cropredy get this extraordinary name? The answer lies on the grass between the car and the hedge on the extreme left. For centuries a preaching cross stood on this site and when the houses were built in the 1960s, the weathered stump of the cross was kept and the road named after its local nickname.

Right Closer to, the remains look more like a cup and spoon than a cup and saucer, but maybe it's in the eye of the beholder. Cropredy goes in for strange street names: nearby are Creampot Lane and the Plantation.

All photographs by the author

11. Wayside inns

The Crown Inn, Chinnor.

CHINNOR: The Crown public house stands, like many inns, at a crossroads, in this case where Station Road crosses Oakley Road and Church Road. The 1960 road was almost clear of markings, and motorists would have just taken 'pot luck' when it came to deciding priority at a quiet junction like this. There's just one roadsign visible, directing drivers to a local beauty spot, the village of Bledlow Ridge in the Chiltern Hills. *OPA*

Thirty years may not have changed the exterior of the Crown very much, but for the road junction it's quite a

different story. In response to an increase in usage, a mini roundabout has been installed, together with traffic islands and lights. Why has traffic increased? The cause is probably the M40. This section of the motorway was finished in 1974 and Junction 6 lies less than five miles from Chinnor.

THAME: A Ford, a Standard, a Morris Oxford and a Land-Rover are just some of the vehicles to be spotted out-side the Spread Eagle Hotel in Thame High Street on this day in the 1960s. The Spread Eagle became well-known in the 1920s because of its owner John Fothergill, described in a blue plaque on the wall of the hotel as 'amateur innkeeper, author, wit and raconteur', but probably best remembered for his legendary rudeness to customers. *OPA*

Pictured on 24 March 1993, Nissans, Vauxhalls and Volvos have replaced the cars of the 'sixties, but the roadscape of the High Street is reassuringly familiar. The Spread Eagle's sturdy inn sign set in the pavement has survived for another thirty years. While in the 1960s there was barely a centre white line in the road, today the traffic lanes are clearly marked and at one point they are separated by an area of diagonal stripes. Pelican crossings have been installed at intervals to help those on foot.

STANTON ST JOHN: The George at Stanton St John on the B4027 just north of Oxford as it looked in March 1969, with a red public phone box handily placed right outside and a Regent petrol station opposite. *OPA*

Another example of how the increase in traffic over the years has led to a junction being marked out more clearly. In this case it seems that the narrow side road beside the George, on the right of the picture, has caused problems. Since 1969 it has been made into a one-way street, and a rectangular white-on-blue arrow sign has been fixed to the side of the pub building. A 'Keep clear' road marking underlines how tricky this turning can be. Though the petrol station has gone and its plot converted into parking for the pub, it's nice to see that the red phone box has been given a reprieve.

WANTAGE: On 8 July 1974 construction work is taking place in Wallingford Street, opposite the Post Office Vaults pub, and two Minis are approaching this rather narrow, twisting junction with the Market Place. *OPA*
   The view of the same junction today, now with pelican lights, shows the completed buildings which house shops and a supermarket. The Post Office Vaults pub has called 'Time!' for the last time - the building is now a shopping mall. Centre white lines and a 'Give way' road marking have been added since 1974.

12. Petrol stations

ENSTONE: Worth's garage was already sixteen years old when this photograph was taken on 10 June 1955. It lies beside the Oxford to Chipping Norton road, then called the A34. This was a grand spot for a bit of advertising and someone has had the enterprising idea of picking out the name of the company in the flower bed. Note also the Esso pumps of the time with their distinctive oval logo, which remains the same today. *OPA*

By 18 August 1981 extensive workshops had been added at the side and the enlarged and remodelled petrol station was serving National petrol. Nevertheless, there was still time to tend to the floral writing and keep it neat. An old-style lamp illuminates the entrance and there is a bus stop right outside. *OPA*

On 9 March 1993 the garage, first begun in 1939, is still in existence, though very changed. Even the road on which it stands has a new designation, the A44. The business today includes coach hire, local bus services, and an MOT testing centre, as well as a Jet petrol station. The lamp has now gone but the ancient bus stop sign is still there. Sadly, expansion of the business has left no room for fancy flower beds.

OVERNORTON: A Ford Escort Estate at Chapel House crossroads on the A361 on 20 November 1970, a nasty wet day by the look of it. The car is about to turn left on to the A34 towards Stratford-upon-Avon. Opposite the junction is an Esso petrol station. *OPA*

In 1993 the petrol station looks the same but, in place of the crossroads, there is now a large roundabout which was completed in June 1973. It's a heavily used junction so considerable street lighting has been installed. With the advent of the M40 the Stratford road has been downgraded to the A3400.

EAST HENDRED: What a difference a decade makes! These pictures and those opposite illustrate the ups and downs of village garages in the 1980s. This one, set in a lane among an attractive row of cottages in East Hendred, with the village church in the background, was photographed on 11 February 1982. *OPA*

By February 1993, like many other village amenities, the garage has disappeared. The building has been converted to a home, and dormer windows added in the roof. The roadscape is unchanged and you can still see the dip in the ancient kerbstones where the archway entrance used to be.

UFFINGTON: A few months earlier, on 28 September 1981 to be precise, the petrol station and garage in Broad Street, Uffington, happened also to be photographed. At the time it was rather a shabby affair, little more than a collection of wooden sheds with tin roofs and one petrol pump. *OPA*

Yes, this is the same place! The ramshackle wooden sheds have been demolished and modern buildings have taken their place; today the village has this splendid garage and car showroom. We can only wonder why the garage at Uffington survived and flourished while the one at East Hendred perished.

Landmarks in postwar British motoring history

The age of the motor car began with the repeal of the Red Flag Act in 1896, and life has never really been the same since. Motor cars made a tremendous impact in the early part of this century and revolutionised the way we lived, but nothing could have prepared us for the dizzying pace of change that has happened in transport since the war, when the dream of cars for the masses became a reality. This time-chart of British motoring landmarks shows just how much has happened on our roads, and in our lives, in the past half a century.

A London traffic warden on patrol in the 1970s.
Metropolitan Police Service

1947   Zebra crossings introduced

1948   First postwar Motor Show held at Earls Court

     Morris Minor produced at Cowley

1950   Petrol rationing ends

     Ford launches Consul and Zephyr range

1952   Blinking beacons on pedestrian crossings become compulsory

1953   Britain's first motel opens in Kent

     Radial-ply tyres marketed

1954   Flashing indicator lights become legal

1955   Jowett closes

     Austin A30 launched

1958   Yellow 'No waiting' lines appear in London

     Parking meters and traffic wardens in London

     First section of motorway, the Preston Bypass, opens

1959   First long-distance motorway, the M1 from London to Birmingham, opens

     Austin and Morris Minis launched

1960   MOTs needed for cars over ten years old

1961   Jaguar introduces the E-type

1961   First self-service petrol pump in operation in London

     Millionth Morris Minor produced

1962   Push-button Panda crossings

     First Ford Cortina

1963   Lord Nuffield (William Morris) dies

1964   New system of traffic signs adopted

1965   Rolls-Royce produces the Silver Shadow

1967   MOTs needed for cars over three years old

     Star grading of petrol introduced

     Breathalyser becomes law

1968   Ford Escort launched

1969   First Pelican crossings

1970   Range Rover launched

1971   Last Morris Minor rolls off the line

1973   Purchase tax on cars abolished - and replaced by VAT

1975 First mini-roundabouts

1977 Ford Fiesta launched

Britain imports more cars than it makes

1980 MG closes

BL Metro launched

1981 First 'gull-winged' De Lorean car appears

1983 Wheel clamps introduced

Wearing of seat belts in front seats becomes law

1985 Clive Sinclair unveils the C5 electric tricycle

1986 Japanese car factory, Nissan, opens in Sunderland

1989 Children under 14 in rear seats must wear seat belts

1991 All rear seat passengers must wear seat belts

These minis have been with us since 1975. *Author*

Since 1991 adult and child rear seat passengers have to be securely belted. *Author*

Every driver's nightmare since 1983 - being clamped. *Metropolitan Police Service*

Index of locations